11-02

To my dear friend Esther
on her 60th birthday.

Lynda

Always Friends

Alda Ellis

WITH HOLLY HALVERSON

HARVEST HOUSE PUBLISHERS

EUGENE, OREGON

Always Friends
Copyright ©1997 Harvest House Publishers
Eugene, Oregon 97402

Library of Congress Cataloging-in-Publication Data
Ellis, Alda,1952-
    Always friends / Alda Ellis.
        p. cm.
    ISBN 1-56507-667-2
    1. Christian women—Biography.   2. Friendship—Religious aspects—
    Christianity—Anecdotes.   3. Female friendship—Anecdotes.   I. Title.
BR1713.E55 1997   97-9438
241'.6762—dc21   CIP

Design and production by Left Coast Design, Portland, Oregon

Artwork which appears in this book is from the personal collection of Alda Ellis.

Scripture quotations are from the Holy Bible, New International Version®.
Copyright ©1973, 1978, 1984 by the International Bible Society. Used by permission of
Zondervan Publishing House.

Printed in Mexico
97 98 99 00 01 02 03 04 05 06 / DR / 10 9 8 7 6 5 4 3 2 1

BIBLIOGRAPHY

Brittain, Vera. *Testament of Friendship*. New York: The Macmillan Company, 1940.

Cheney, Ednah D. *Louisa May Alcott: Her Life, Letters and Journals*. Boston: Little,
Brown, and Company, 1928.

Keller, Helen. *The Story of My Life*. New York: Dell Publishing Co., Inc., 1902.

Raymond, Meredith B. and Mary Rose Sullivan, eds. *Women of Letters: Selected
Letters of Elizabeth Barrett Browning and Mary Russell Mitford*. Boston: Twayne
Publishers, 1987.

ten Boom, Corrie and John and Elizabeth Sherrill. *The Hiding Place*. Uhrichsville,
OH: Barbour and Company, Inc., 1971.

*D*edicated to my husband,

who after all these twenty-one years

of marriage is still my best friend.

Contents

Count your blessings
By smiles, not tears
Count your age
By friends, not years.

Friendships have been treasured throughout the ages as one of God's greatest gifts. Friendship unites our feelings, binds our hearts, and melds two souls into one. True friendship is unwavering; whether cultivated across the backyard fence or kept across the miles, best friends are never parted.

In these pages you will find six stories of extraordinary friendships, kindred spirits finding each other in unimaginable circumstances, meant-to-be best friends sharing hearts in homespun beginnings. In each true story, we see the way companions soften the hard edges of life and make dim hope a palpable reality. Elizabeth Barrett Browning and Mary Russell Mitford were true friends by letters bound, whose warm correspondence formed a tie that reached over years, distance, and tragedy; Annie Sullivan lifted Helen Keller's shroud of silence and connected her to the world; Corrie and Betsie ten Boom were sustained in a World War II prison camp by sisterly devotion and a common faith; Ruth and Naomi clasped hands when bitterness would separate them, only to witness their mutual and divine renewal; Winifred Holtby realized her heavenly appointment to soothe her friend Vera Brittain through hardship into a thriving life, and from shattering losses rose a rich gathering of joys.

Take a moment to value the friendships in your own life. Who has offered you that timely word, the tender nudge of truth when you most needed it? Who has whispered confidences meant for your ear only, and encouraged you to dream grand dreams? Have you been changed by the consistency of a true companion? How can you affect someone else today with the love you have received?

It was on a trip to London that four friends and I discovered the endearing tradition of the Friendship Ball. An age-old ritual, the Ball (containing small gifts as special chocolates, a pretty pin, antique buttons, a recipe, or a lacy handkerchief) passed between friends in times of need and on occasions of affection. Its contents mattered less than the Ball itself: The true gift, you see, was the friendship that it carried.

A ball is a circle,
No beginning, no end.
It keeps us together
Like our circle of friends.
But the treasure inside,
For you just to see,
Is the treasure of friendship
You've granted to me.

Today, I pass the Friendship Ball to you. Who in your life could be cheered by it? Be looking for someone else who needs it. It's your turn to pass it on.

Each friend represents a world in us, a world possibly not born until they arrive, and it is only by this meeting that a new world is born.

ANAIS NIN

A Sky
Made Radiant
by a Sun

Helen Keller and Annie Sullivan

The most important day I remember in all my life is the one on which my teacher, Anne Mansfield Sullivan, came to me," wrote Helen Keller. *Wrote* Helen Keller. The word itself introduces the marvel of one of womenkind's most brilliant friendships, for without Annie Sullivan's devoted and unwavering attachment, Helen may never have marked history at all.

Rendered deaf, blind, and speechless by a fever just months before her second birthday, Helen Keller

lived in "a tangible white darkness" until March 3, 1887.
With the arrival of a patient new teacher, Miss Sullivan,
came the priceless gifts of discipline, instructive love, and
relentless encouragement. It was by these gifts that six-
year-old Helen was rescued from her world of darkness.

The first lesson the teacher taught was obedience.
Helen had been a wild, unruly girl, given to fits of tem-
per. Annie knew she
could teach nothing
without the attention
of her learner, so
she bequeathed to
her pupil the
saving graces
of responding
appropriately
to yes and no. It
was the beginning
of a mutual
respect. Once
young Helen
became obliging

and teachable, the pair graduated to spelling words. From there Helen made the discovery that would usher her into a radiant new world: "Everything has a name." Suddenly gestures had meaning. Objects had labels. And feelings could be described and shared with others.

This extraordinary woman who guided her pupil as both teacher and friend desired most of all for Helen to understand the concept of love. Early in their relationship Annie put her arm around the little girl and signed into her hand, "I love Helen." Puzzled, Helen asked what love was. She wondered if love were the smell of violets or the warmth of the sun. No, the teacher patiently explained. "You cannot touch love . . . but you can feel the sweetness that it pours into everything. Without love you would not be happy or want to play."

Again Helen felt the world burst into her being— and this time, it was peopled. "I felt that there were invisible lines stretched between my spirit and the spirits of others," she exulted.

Connecting Helen to the world and folks around her was miraculous. Perhaps equally so was Helen's teacher. Annie Sullivan's background was bleak. First, a childhood illness had left her partially blind; she never fully recovered her sight. Later she survived life in a brutal almshouse, where she was sent at age ten. Nothing in such a background suggests its survivor would be willing or able to teach another about love, yet love was Annie's specialty.

Of their mutual attachment Helen wrote in her autobiography—another treasure made possible by Annie

Sullivan's gifts of time and patience—"My teacher is so near to me that I can scarcely think of myself apart from her. . . . All the best of me belongs to her—there is not a talent, or an aspiration or a joy in me that has not been awakened by her loving touch."

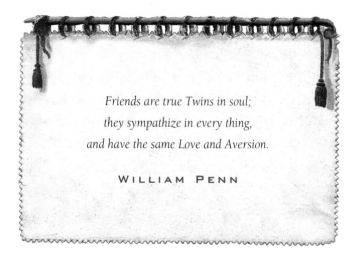

Friends are true Twins in soul;
they sympathize in every thing,
and have the same Love and Aversion.

WILLIAM PENN

There is no friend like a sister

In calm or stormy weather;

To cheer one on the tedious way,

To fetch one if one goes astray,

To lift one if one totters down,

To strengthen whilst one stands.

CHRISTINA ROSSETTI

16

A Shining Light in the Dark

Corrie and Betsie ten Boom

Though seven years separated them in age, Corrie ten Boom and her older sister Betsie were identical twins in purpose. Both loved deeply and took watchful care of their family and their business. Corrie specialized in bookkeeping and assisting her father in their watch-repair shop. Betsie excelled in making their Amsterdam home pleasant and welcoming, always keeping a simmering pot of soup on the stove for the homeless who often stopped in for a meal that nourished body and spirit

alike. Together the sisters lived a full life that included various aunts, nieces, nephews, and siblings . . . and eventually, more dangerous citizens.

As Hitler ravaged Europe in the 1940s, Jews sought refuge wherever they could to avoid the terror of the concentration camps. The ten Booms, sturdy in faith and strong in obedience, quickly transformed their rambling old home into a welcome refuge for Jewish friends and neighbors. Corrie selflessly shared a hidden section of her bedroom as a hiding place for them, at least five at a time.

After much success at saving Jewish lives, the day arrived when the ten Boom hiding place was discovered, and the family was unmercifully arrested for their "crimes." It was at this point of deepest darkness that Betsie shone so bright. Always the sweeter of the sisters, Corrie felt,

Betsie met her captors with an uncommon compassion. After an officer beat her for withholding information, Betsie told her sister, "I feel so sorry for him." Then the middle-aged siblings and their elderly father were taken to prison. When they faced their first separation in fifty-three years, Betsie took Corrie's hand. She held it—in spirit—every day that followed.

Corrie's first days in the cold, dank prison cell were made hazy by fever. She suffered long, lonely hours on a rancid cot with a racking cough and troubling thoughts: Where was Father? Betsie? Were they all right? Were the Jews they had hidden free or had they been captured? What of the rest of their closely knit family?

Finally, word came. The Jews were safe. All of their family members except Betsie and Corrie had been

released to home; their father, to heaven, just ten days after his arrest. And then, perhaps, the most needed news of all: "Betsie ten Boom is in cell 312. She says to tell you God is good."

Moved to another camp to continue their sentence, the sisters were joyfully reunited. Still, camp life proved brutal. One day Corrie cried out her frustration: "How long?" Betsie's words shone like a flare in the midnight sky: "Perhaps many years. But what better way could there be to spend our lives?"

Corrie stared in disbelief. "Whatever are you talking about?"

"These young women," Betsie answered. "Corrie, if people can be taught to hate, they can be taught to love! We must find the way. . . ."

Corrie slowly realized that Betsie was speaking of their guards.

Finally Betsie's always delicate health succumbed to the pains of prison life. As a stretcher carried her to the infirmary, Betsie whispered last instructions to Corrie: " . . . must tell people what we have learned here. We must tell them that there is no pit so deep that He is not deeper still. . . ." Betsie ten Boom died the next day, her emaciated form softened by peace; hunger, grief, and worry permanently exchanged for eternal joy.

Within weeks, Corrie was released from prison. True to her long-loved sister's wishes, Corrie went on to tell an international audience of her experience and deliverance in prison camp. She saw the fulfillment of Betsie's wish: homes for those wounded by imprisonment, innocents and betrayers alike. And

Corrie's story of "the hiding place"
always included the account of faithful Betsie, her partner in living and giving life.

Who is it that stands beside you when
darkness falls? Hold fast to her hand, and thank
her for her sisterly love.

With every friend I love who has been taken into the brown
bosom of the earth a part of me has been buried there; but
their contribution to my being of happiness, strength and
understanding remains to sustain me in an altered world.

HELEN KELLER

Friendship is
something that raises us
almost above humanity. . . .
It is the sort
of love one can imagine
between angels.

C.S. LEWIS

A Paper Bond the Strongest

Elizabeth Barrett Browning and Mary Russell Mitford

*T*he reams of paper, bottles of ink, immeasurable; the affection passed between writers Elizabeth Barrett Browning and Mary Russell Mitford, inestimable, yet rich and meaningful as life itself. Introduced by a mutual friend, Elizabeth initiated a lasting correspondence with Mary, who was nineteen years her senior. Exchanges of literary opinions and collaborations gave way eventually to most personal declarations as to each woman's state of health and heart. Their letters carried no less the news of the day, including a trip to view the Queen, the account

of a party at which Charles Dickens made a vivid appearance, and a visit with the notorious female figure, George Sand. Throughout their nearly two decades of letter writing, Elizabeth and Mary revealed the power of what the written words of kindred spirits can accomplish: convey love, strengthen hope, and form an intimate and unbreakable friendship that transcends the barriers of distance and age.

The colleagues and friends guided each other through many changes in their personal circumstances: moving to different cities and countries, death (Mary's father, Elizabeth's brother), illness (both women suffered uncertain health), professional successes, Elizabeth's marriage to her beloved poet Robert Browning, and mutual seasons of rest. Mary and Elizabeth shared a love for animals, and this bond too found expression in correspondence, in Mary's vivid description of her dogs' mishaps and Elizabeth's tender nursing of her pet doves. When Elizabeth was devastated by the cruel loss of her brother,

Mary sent her a puppy, Flush, who brightened many a day and became a major part of many letters.

In fact it was in tragedy where letters proved to be more than paper but carriers for courage. After "Bro's" death, Elizabeth wrote:

My beloved friend,

You have not thought me ill or—worse still—unkind, for not writing?— I feel bound more than I ever remember having felt, in chains, heavy & cold enough to be iron—& which have indeed entered into the soul. But I do love you still—& am rather better than worse— likely, I do suppose to live on. In the meantime, thank you thank you for your letter, & both of you Dr. Mitford [Mary's father], & my beloved friend, for your affectionate sympathy. . . . Your unchangingly affectionate EBB—

The depth of feeling that laced
the scratching of quill upon page
warmed each reader through the
wintry breezes and late springs of
time and life. Every fond epistle
contained exclamations of and
entreaties to love.

"How my Love for you has
been pulling at my sleeve these two days,
to write. . . ."

"It haunts me that you are suffering."

"Believe, my beloved friend, how near I
am to you in thought, in prayer, in sympathy of
tender affection."

"I am alone; that is the thought that clings to me,
though when I think of you, sister of my heart, it
presses less heavily. . . ."

"Love me, my beloved friend! And write
& say if I can do anything, supply you with
anything. . . ."

And so words
flew, from writer to

recipient, from mind to mind, from heart to heart. From their meeting until Mary's death in 1855, Mary and Elizabeth shared a friendship forged of nothing less than the crossed hearts and shared souls of deepest friendship. And so the strength of their intimacy upheld them both.

Who holds a piece of your heart? Perhaps you can share your fondness in a special letter and seal it with love.

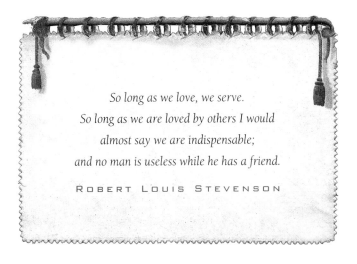

So long as we love, we serve.
So long as we are loved by others I would
almost say we are indispensable;
and no man is useless while he has a friend.

ROBERT LOUIS STEVENSON

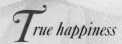

True happiness

Consists not in

the multitude of friends,

But in the worth

and the choice.

BEN JONSON

On the
Path to
Friendship

Vera Brittain and Winifred Holtby

S ometimes the bond of friendship forms instantly;
other times, two must make hesitant strides
toward discovering each other before the sunlight
of friendship can burst through. Writer Vera Brittain
found the latter true of her first encounter with the viva-
cious novelist Winifred Holtby in 1920s England. "We
did not, to begin with, like each other at all," she states
bluntly in the biography she later wrote for Winifred,
Testament of Friendship.

Part of the initial barrier for Vera rose from a suc-
cession of losses that left her love-shy. War had stolen the
lives of her fiancé, brother, and his two best friends.
Vera's deep melancholy and woundedness initially
clashed with Winifred's exuberance and sprightly energy.
A school term later, however, the young women found
themselves gently drawn together, and over studies and
long walks, they slowly built the foundation of a compan-
ionship that ran largely uninterrupted for sixteen years.

The women's contributions to each other's lives
were profound. Winifred's quiet but con-
tinual prompting saw the
publication of Vera's
first book, a long-
wrought dream.
Vera's children
replaced the
ones Winifred
was never able to
bear. They shared
the trials of romance,
the discouragement of ill

health, and, for two separate, happy periods, the perils and triumphs of housekeeping.

Renting a flat together in London allowed the blossoming of common comfort. Vera and Winifred enjoyed a relationship that eventually became intuitive; thoughts overlapped, unspoken requests were granted. This synergy served them especially well when illness gradually entered Winifred's life. Vera easily took over her friend's voluminous correspondence and corrected her articles and story proofs; their minds, she noted, were "virtually interchangeable."

Vera credited Winifred with an exquisitely developed generosity that gave her endurance through Vera's early trials and frustrations as a writer. Winifred admitted she felt herself a "debtor to life," owing to the fact that life had blessed her with little suffering. She felt naturally obligated to give immeasurably to those she saw as less fortunate. Vera touched her life equally deeply, though,

as Winifred wrote:

> *"I find you in all small*
> *and lovely things; in the*
> *little fishes like flames*
> *in the green water,*
> *in the furred and stupid*
> *softness of bumble-bees*
> *fat as laughter,*
> *in all the chiming radiance*
> *of warmth and light*
> *and scent in the*
> *summer garden."*

For her part, after death took Winifred at age thirty-seven, Vera wrote of her friend:

> *"No one, least of all myself,*
> *is worth such pure rarity of devoted love.*
> *No treasure in heaven or earth can replace it,*
> *or atone for its loss."*

Flowers are lovely; Love is flower-like;
Friendship is a sheltering tree;
O! the joys, that came down shower-like,
Of Friendship, Love, and Liberty.

SAMUEL TAYLOR COLERIDGE

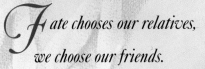

F ate chooses our relatives,
we choose our friends.

JACQUES DELILLE

A Friendship Bound with Faith

Ruth and Naomi

One wonders what Naomi thought when Ruth, a foreigner, joined her family as a daughter-in-law. Did she hesitate to welcome her? Was she concerned that Ruth would draw her husband away from his family's faith? Did she glimpse at all the precious devotion that would bring her renewal when she most needed it?

About the early days of Naomi and Ruth's relationship, we know only that tragedy swept the family, leaving them both without husband or child. In Naomi's heartache, she blessed her daughter-in-law and entreated

her to return to the security of her homeland, away from
her great despair. But Ruth met Naomi's good-bye kiss
with grief of her own, refusing to be parted from her. At
the point of Naomi's deepest loss, Ruth spoke some of
the Bible's most cherished words:

"Where you go, I will go, and where you stay I will stay.
Your people will be my people, and your God my God."

Lacking the strength or will to
plead with Ruth further, Naomi
accepted her commit-
ment and compan-
ionship, and the
pair traveled to
Bethlehem.
There
sorrow hollowed
Naomi's heart.
The whole town
marveled at her
darkened counte-
nance. She appealed
to her neighbors to

call her Mara, meaning "bitter," rather than Naomi, which meant "pleasant." Her faith in a good God weakened, Naomi's hope withered.

In her deep sorrow, she never imagined how close help was. One day Ruth asked Naomi's permission to glean in the grain fields, a great risk to a foreign woman both young and alone. There her beauty captured the attention of the field's kindhearted owner, Boaz, who quietly saw to her safety and increased her harvest by asking his servants to drop extra grain in her path. He fed her. He watched her. And he wondered about her.

Asking his foreman her identity, Boaz learned of Ruth's dedication to her mother-in-law. He blessed her for her service, which she accepted with humility.

When Ruth arrived home that night, Naomi exclaimed over her bountiful gleanings. Ruth told her of Boaz and his kindness.

Ruth continued to glean in the barley and wheat fields, as Naomi wished, until the harvests were finished.

Then Naomi sought
Ruth's heart: "Should I not try to
find a home for you, where you will
be well provided for?" she asked.
Boaz's continued benevolence had struck
a chord in the widow's heart, and she saw in him
a devoted, faithful husband for her former
daughter-in-law. She told Ruth to go seek Boaz's
favor. Ruth, proclaiming her love and respect for
Naomi, replied: "I will do whatever you say."

She did. That night, she spoke kindly to Boaz, asking him to take her into his household. Deeply impressed
by this gracious young woman, Boaz replied in blessing.
"You have not run after the younger men, whether rich or
poor," he observed. Boaz would take Ruth for his own.
He gave Ruth barley for Naomi, and sent her home.

Ruth became a devoted wife to Boaz and later, the
mother of their son.

The same neighbors who had remarked upon
Naomi's bitterness now rejoiced in her good fortune.
They celebrated the God who provided for her. They
cherished the young woman whose loyalty brought hap-

piness and security to them both. And they sang praises: "Your daughter-in-law . . . loves you and . . . is better to you than seven sons."

So the woman who entered Naomi's house simply as a foreigner left her house as a rare and precious friend, bringing Naomi blessings both times. She exchanged bitter for sweet, and tragic loss for fullness of joy.

A faithful friend is the medicine of life.

ECCLESIASTES 9:10

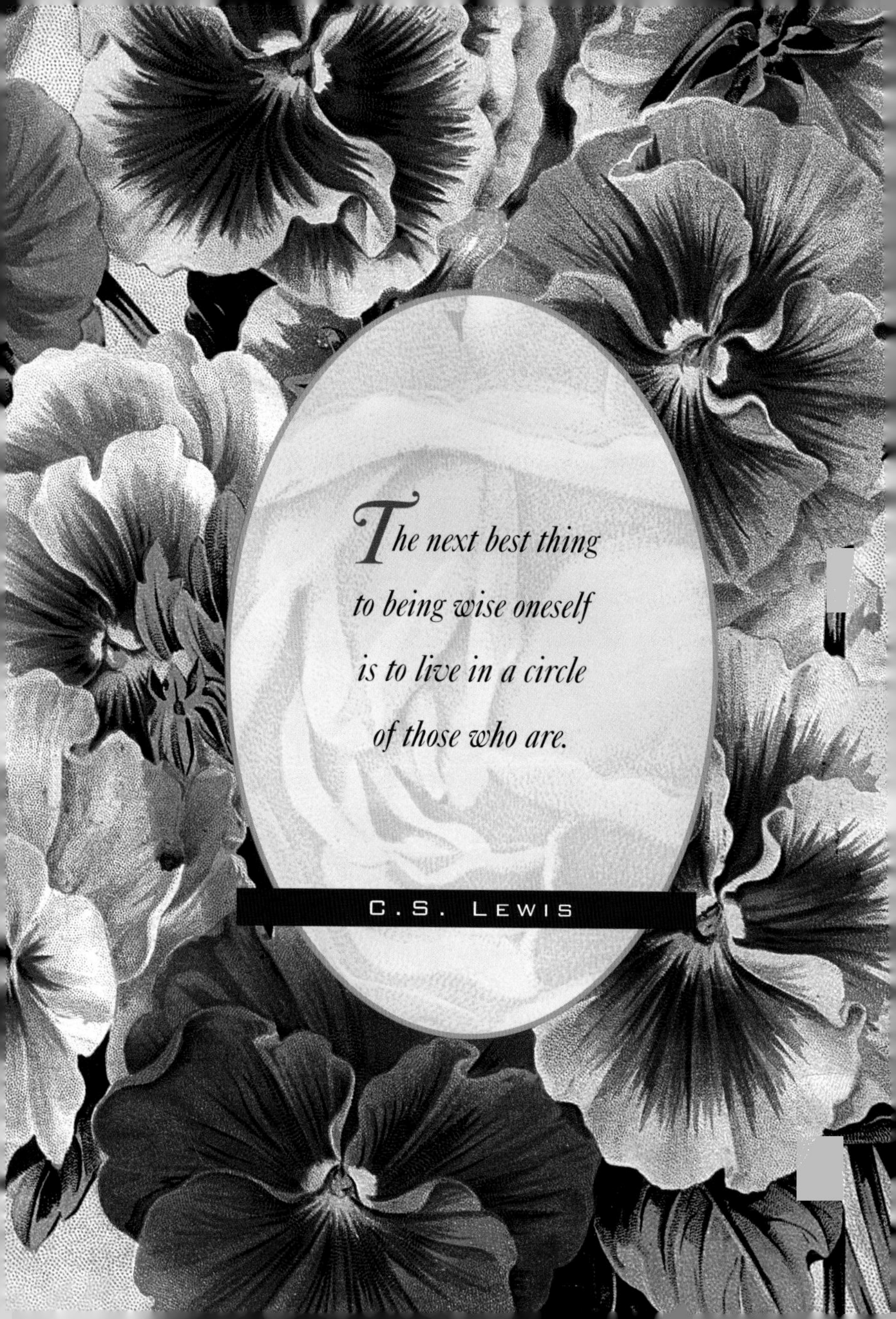

*T*he next best thing

to being wise oneself

is to live in a circle

of those who are.

C.S. LEWIS

A Friendship Like No Other

Louisa May Alcott and Her Mother, Abba May Alcott

Louisa May Alcott's beloved rendition of family life, *Little Women*, was based largely on her own. Of the March family characters, among the most easily identified are Jo and Marmee, Louisa and Abba May, respectively. Years after the book's publication, the author admitted to the inquisitive, "Mrs. March is all true, only not half so good." By Louisa's own account, the real Marmee was a woman of full devotion who modeled for her children the best humanity can offer to God. In this she served as not only mother but best friend, for her training well prepared Louisa for the demanding and fulfilling life ahead of her.

Thanks to her mother's sparkling example, Louisa could look back on her life satisfied that she had cared well for the numerous bright spirits who peopled her world—a deep gratification, indeed.

Mrs. Alcott was a woman of great energy and loving discipline. Giving seemed to be not just her hobby but her lifework, and her beneficiaries included many outside the family home. At one point she served as a professional "visitor" to the poor, yet the same quality of concern marked her "nonprofessional" activities. Mrs. Alcott also appreciated thoughts transferred to paper, and Louisa and her sisters drew strength from many small notes of encouragement during their growing-up years. One can hear the echoes of the beloved Marmee March in such sentiments as: "Dear Daughter, Your tenth birthday has arrived. May it be a happy one, and on each returning birthday may you feel new strength and resolution to be gentle with sisters, obedient to parents,

loving to every one, and happy in yourself." Louisa's response, here recorded in a poem entitled "Mother," shows she shared the embrace her mother offered, and she dreamt often of the day:

> *While I sit close beside you,*
> *Content at last to see*
> *That you can rest, dear Mother,*
> *And I can cherish thee.*

While the Alcotts, like the March family, enjoyed four daughters, a special thread seemed to tie Louisa to her mother. Mrs. Alcott once gave Louisa the gift of a little picture, entreating her, "Keep it for my sake and your own, for you and I always liked to be grouped together." Louisa faithfully recorded in her journal the motherly advice she received "to show the ever tender, watchful help she gave to the child who caused her the most anxiety, yet seemed to be the nearest to her heart till the end."

As Louisa grew

into a successful authoress and a busy patron of others herself, it was her mother's model she clung to in word and deed. Mrs. Alcott's compassion for the less fortunate blossomed equally as full in her daughter, who taught at a charity school, reasoning, "I'll help as I'm helped, if I can. Mother says no one [is] so poor he can't do a little for some one poorer yet." Louisa often practiced Mrs. Alcott's habit of exchanging discouragement for work.

When a sister died shortly after childbirth and Louisa became custodian of her niece, who was, appropriately, named Louisa May, Marmee Alcott's example was best put to use. As Louisa raised the child, she hearkened often to the loving childhood she remembered, in which Mother proved always a solace to daughter, as well as guide, protector, and friend.

In Mrs. Alcott's last days, Louisa was deeply gladdened by the opportunity to serve her mother as she had

been served. The rich rewards of her productive working years allowed her to provide the restful atmosphere for Mrs. Alcott that she had dreamed of since a little girl. The elderly mother rested in her daughter's attentive care, asking only, "Stay by, Louy, and help me if I suffer too much." After her mother's passing in 1878, so completely had a light extinguished for Louisa that she wrote, "I think I shall soon follow her, and am quite ready to go now she no longer needs me." Fortunately, Louisa lived another decade, in which she honored her mother's legacy by characteristically caring for her family and penning many more delightful stories, including the popular addendum to *Little Women, Jo's Boys*.

As allies and friends whose lives celebrated the best in each other, Louisa and Mrs. Alcott were tributes to a life well lived. When searching for cherished companions, look first to those closest. The nearest may prove dearest after all.

> *There is in friendship something of all relations, and something above them all. It is the golden thread that ties the heart of all the world.*
>
> JOHN EVELYN

*M*y only sketch, profile, of Heaven is a large blue
sky, and larger than the biggest I have seen in June—and in it
are my friends—all of them—every one of them.

EMILY DICKINSON

*T*hrough these stories we have tasted the refreshing
sweetness of the friendships of women: loyal, self-sacrificing,
life-changing. Did you see reflections of much-loved friends
in these accounts? Did you sense a longing to be a
friend like these you have read about?

By all means, reach out. Seize each opportunity to embrace
another in friendship. As these stories reveal, your touch may
leave a lasting mark, one that ignites the courage borne
of the love of a friend. Love will be your reward,
and many will eat the fruit that results.